No	002
Date	/ /
Name	
Season	

@getmessyartjournal | getmessyart.com

Welcome, collage

This idea book is for you if you're going from creative dabbler to artsy practice-r or if you feel like the art you're making just doesn't look quite like you'd like it to. Overall, it's to level up the products and classes you have and learn to rely on yourself.

THIS IS MODERN ART JOURNALING.

Back in the good old days, before the internet and Wikipedia, we had encyclopedias. The knowledge of the entire universe (or so we thought) is housed in 32 volumes of thick, sturdy books.

These Idea Books bring back that nostalgia and endeavor to cover a broad array of art journaling techniques. Definitely not all of them, but certainly enough so that you'll never be stuck on what to do next.

WE DO THIS IN THE FORM OF GET MESSY *Recipes*

This type of art journaling format has been around for over a **DECADE** and has been tried and tested. Messy Recipes have magical properties.

I liken Messy Recipes to baking a cake because they have ingredients (the art supplies) and a method. They're also totally not like baking a cake though, because you don't have to keep things exact. In fact, you're encouraged not to. When following a Messy Recipe, follow your curiosity, adapt, branch out, ignore certain things, and absolutely follow your joy.

Every single time you follow a recipe, you'll discover a new outcome. If you're lucky enough to have creative friends, try following along together (our favorite thing we do in the Get Messy community. Marvel at how, even with the exact same ingredients and method, the outcomes vary so wildly and beautifully.

The other magical part of Messy Recipes? They prevent overthinking and allow you to just have fun in your art. Learn new techniques, **MAKE A MESS**, release expectations, and enjoy the process.

Are you willing to try? Have all the stuff? Let's get over that hump, grab our (paint-soaked) hands, and take action.

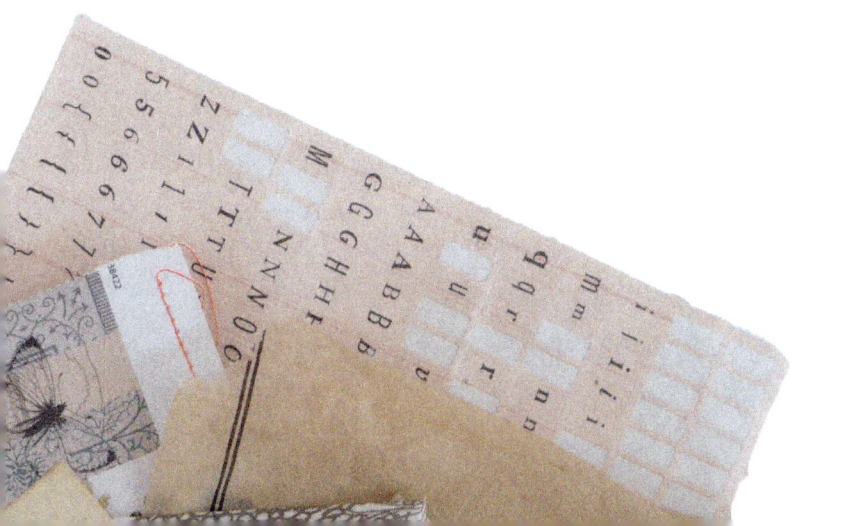

WELCOME TO THE VERY FIRST GET MESSY IDEA BOOK.

Collage

Collage is a staple for so many art journalers because it allows us to indulge in our magpie-ness. We get to put those papers collected over time and put them in use in the journal.

> "We are mosaics. Pieces of light, love, history, stars... glued together with Magic + Music + Words"
>
> — ANITA KRIZZAN

In the same way that we are multi-faceted, collage allows our journal to be too. There is creativity imbued in every step of the process - collecting, arranging, and placing. Choose images that spark something deep within you to create another facet representing who you are.

You'll learn from three very different artists (Caylee, Claudette, and Vanessa), and you'll get to discover your style through it. We'll guide you gently and enthusiastically. We'll show you the technique and how to make it your own.

Let's release the art that looks like you.

Techniques

PG 1 — **THE ALTERED FIGURE:**
Make magazine images your own

PG 11 — **USING A FOCAL IMAGE:**
Expand outward to create a cohesive spread

PG 19 — **A WEEK IN PAPER:**
Collect pieces of life through paper and store them in your journal

PG 27 — **MORE IS MORE LAYERING:**
Add more and more layers to create depth

PG 35 — **PEEK & REVEAL:**
Allow the unexpected to guide your flow to reveal what lies beneath

PG 45 — **LAYERING TRANSPARENCIES:**
Play with papers of varying opacities

PG 53 — **BONUS:**
Collage as Expression

SAY HI TO YOUR ARTISTS!

CAYLEE GREY

Hyperbolic journaler and imperfect artist, Caylee Grey is also a wife and mother from South Africa. Caylee is the Fairy Artmother of the Get Messy art journal community, book, and art supplies brand. She has sworn an oath to embrace the messy middle and believes that more than zero is enough.

CLAUDETTE HASENJAGER

Claudette Hasenjager is a mixed-media artist living in sunny South Africa. She firmly believes that art has the power to heal and nurture the soul. Her art reflects the many facets of her inner landscape and gives expression to her multi-passionate personality. It is this deep calling from within that has fueled her passion for exploring various forms of creative expression. Through her art and her creative process, she strives to inspire others to heed the call of their own unique creative yearning, free their artist soul, and find comfort and healing through developing their own art practice.

VANESSA OLIVER-LLOYD

Vanessa is a Canadian artist who lives abroad. This has lead her to explore art as a way of connecting and engaging with the world. She loves to share what she learns in classes that speak directly from the heart.

BONUS

ALYSSA GRIESE

Living in Canada, with a BA in visual arts, Alyssa is a maker and lover of all things handmade. Art Journaling captured her heart only a few shorts years ago and quickly became a passion and daily source of inspiration and creativity. For Alyssa, embracing imperfections and chasing after "happy accidents" is the true magic of art journaling. Anything goes within the pages of her art journal and it has become an important place for her to process, to experiment and to play.

LESSON ONE:

altered figure

MAKE MAGAZINE IMAGES YOUR OWN

When I use magazine figures within my spreads, altering them in some way allows me to make them more my own. It helps make them feel more like art and further integrated into my spread.

ART TEACHER:
CLAUDETTE HASENJAGER

CORE TECHNIQUE:
Making figures your own

Ingredients

- Your magazine figure
- Collage pieces to alter your figure with - these can include found words, thread, and small ephemera pieces
- Your favorite collage adhesive

METHOD

STEP 1: Start by choosing your figure. Knowing what your figure looks like will help with selecting your collage pieces for your background because you will have a clearer idea of the story you will be creating.

STEP 2: Glue down your collage pieces to create your background, and then add your figure to your landscape.

STEP 3: Now the magic of altering your figure can begin. Don't be afraid to try new things, add cut-out ephemera elements, stickers, and more. This is where you can have some fun and create your very own characters.

STEP 4: For this figure, I decided to cover her eyes with some found words, and a neon yellow star to alter her face. I added a heart created by one of my hand-carved stamps, and blood, or teardrops, cut from one of my monoprints. I wanted to bring even more focus to the figure, so I added some threads radiating out from the heart.

To finish her transformation, I decided to add a butterfly wing.

Make it your own

- To make this alteration process even more personal, use elements that you have created instead of using only printed elements for your alterations.
- Draw or paint directly onto your figures to create your alterations.
- Use parts from other figures, or animals, to transform your figure.

try wings, antlers, ears or tails

CAYLEE'S TAKE:

VANESSA'S TAKE:

YOUR TAKE:

LESSON TWO:
Using a Focal Image

EXPAND OUTWARD TO CREATE A COHESIVE SPREAD

This method allows us to expand outward from one or two bigger focal images and create a spread that is cohesive visually and thematically. It is also an easy method that can be applied in mediums or techniques other than collage.

ART TEACHER:
VANESSA OLIVER-LLOYD

CORE TECHNIQUE:
Using a magazine image as a jumping off point for your spread

Ingredients

- Art journal
- 1-2 bigger magazine images
- Watercolors (or media of choice)
- Smaller paper pieces
- Markers, paint pens, black pen
- Glue
- Scissors

Method

STEP 1: Gather your materials, including one or two bigger magazine images with a central figure on them. Choose at least one that has a lot of color. Pull out some smaller pieces or another image that you can cut down if need be. In my case, I have two images: the colorful floral man and the darker woman.

STEP 2: Figure out how you want your focal image(s) to lay on the page. Here are a few variations that I looked at.

The idea here is to see what layout best expresses what you are trying to say while also being aesthetically pleasing. I decided to place the two images almost interlocking like this.

STEP 3: Now take a look at your colorful image and find the colors that you want to work with. I matched the colors with my set of shimmering watercolors, but you can use whatever medium works best for you (and that you have on hand). I went ahead and made waves of color using two shades of pink, a pale green, a pale golden yellow and a dark blue.

STEP 4: Glue down your focal images, now we will work to change up the images to make them our own. Lay down some of the smaller collage elements that you have pulled out. I used some butterflies and punched circles. Try to have these smaller pieces match the same color scheme as your colorful focal image. I like to lay down these pieces to help transform what the magazine images look like.

STEP 5: Once you have a good idea of where you would like to place your smaller pieces, use your paint or gel pens to further transform the magazine images. In my case, I drew around the eyes of the darker figure as well as texturing her hair.

STEP 6: I added more line work to further transform the initial images. I worked with the symbolism of the stars and butterflies. I drew lined waves using different pens that went from the colorful figure's mouth outward and from the darker figure's hair toward the butterfly. It reminds me of an Anais Nin quote: My hair is being pulled by the stars again.

STEP 7: To tie the whole spread together, I added the journaling according to what I am expressing here, which is the notion of change and transformation. So, even as we went from using a certain image, we transformed it and created something new from it.

Make it your own

Instead of using watercolor to pull the colors from your focal image, try using paper to find the matching colors. Using paint sample cards is a free and easy way to do this.

CLAUDETTE'S TAKE:

CAYLEE'S TAKE:

YOUR TAKE:

LESSON THREE:

A Week in Paper

COLLECT PIECES OF LIFE THROUGH PAPER
AND STORE THEM IN YOUR JOURNAL

Over a decade ago, when I was still blogging and before I started art journaling, I shared something I called "A Week in Paper." I scanned in various pieces of paper I had collected throughout my week and shared that unfiltered image. It gave those papers importance and it transported me directly back to the time the tiny bit of paper came into my life.

Let's collect pieces of life through paper and store them in your journal.

ART TEACHER:
CAYLEE GREY

CORE TECHNIQUE:
Using found papers

Ingredients

- Papers from life - business cards, invoices and receipts, paper menus, handwritten notes, gift wrap, packaging, offcuts from creating, grocery lists, sticky notes, school homework or meeting notes, junk mail, forms, brochures, envelopes, stamps, stickers
- Acrylic paint and a brush
- Glue - a stick or tape runner

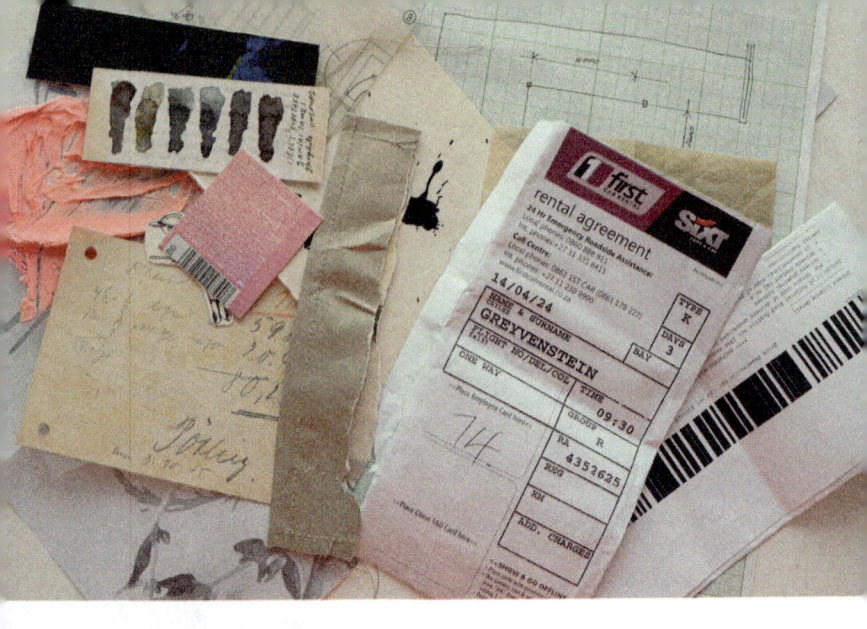

METHOD

STEP 1: Start with the largest piece of paper you have and use it to cover the whole page so that there's no white left.

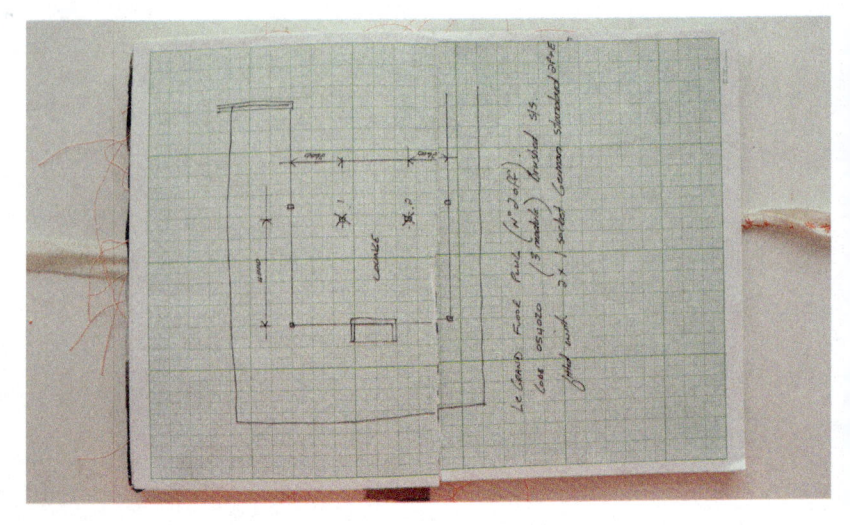

STEP 2: Tear a piece off the next largest and cover about a quarter of your page.

Bonus points for creating a deckled edge

STEP 3: Add another piece on both sides of the journal.

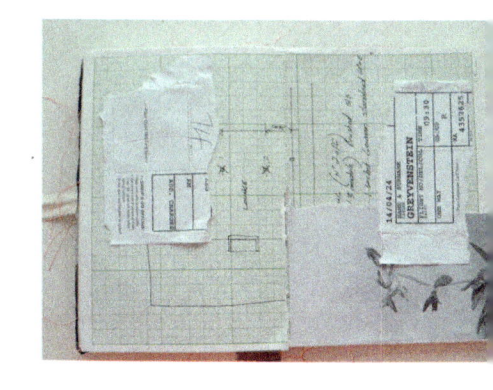

STEP 4: Continue adding the paper from your week. Don't glue the edges of the paper because you may want to tuck something underneath it later.

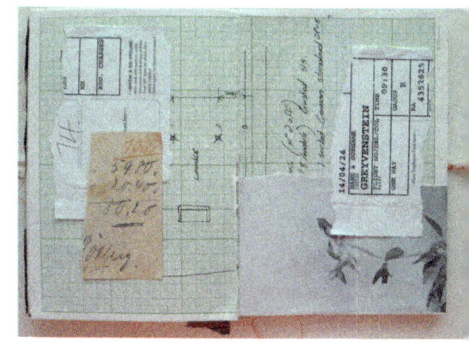

STEP 5: Keep going - work on the outer edges. Create symmetry by adding the paper on both sides.

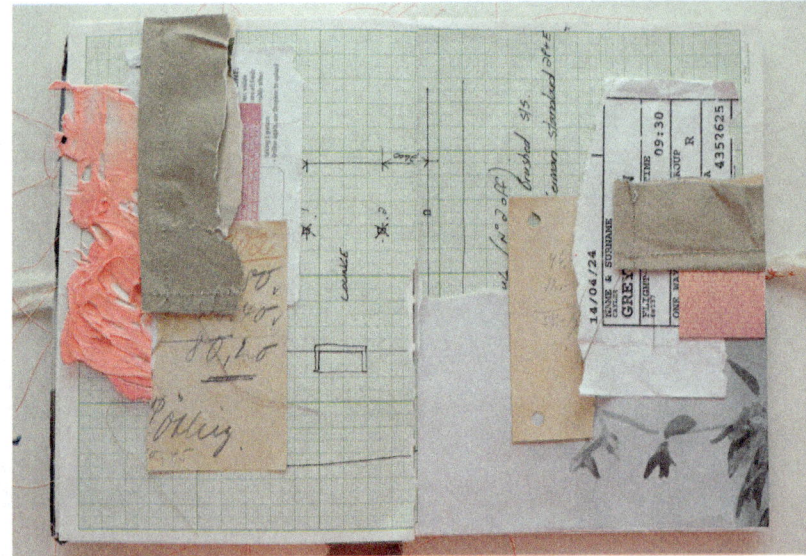

STEP 6: Once you have a nice collection on each side of the crease, choose one of the papers left over and write something on it with acrylic paint.

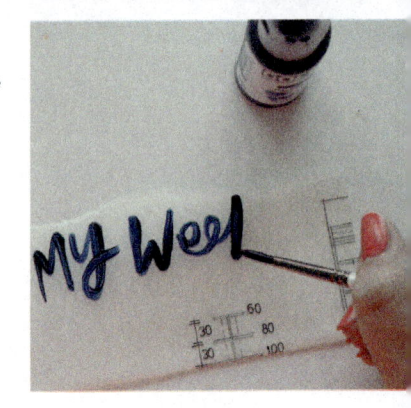

STEP 7: Add that to the center of your spread (cut it in half if you need to) and allow it to bring the spread together.

Make it your own

- Look for a color theme amongst your found papers
- Place your handwritten word or phrase on the sides or use a different medium instead of acrylic paint.

I love adding old paint palettes into a collage

CLAUDETTE'S TAKE:

VANESSA'S TAKE:

YOUR TAKE:

LESSON FOUR:

More is More Layering

ADD MORE AND MORE
LAYERS TO CREATE DEPTH

I love having people question what came first, how things are layered up, or where one piece ends and another begins.

ART TEACHER:
CLAUDETTE HASENJAGER

CORE TECHNIQUE:
Making figures your own

Ingredients

- Collage pieces
- Your favorite collage adhesive
- Paints
- Inks
- Markers

METHOD

STEP 1: Start your spread by selecting your collage pieces to create your color story. Choose pieces you love and that have interest and variation within them. You are going to be working on blending these pieces, so you want to find them visually interesting.

STEP 2: Once you have arranged the placement of your paper pieces get them glued down using your favorite collage adhesive.

STEP 3: Use paints, inks, and markers start blending your papers to create your paper landscape. Keep layering marks, supplies, and paper pieces until you are happy with how your pieces are merged.

Take your time with this.

- Use paints that have similar colors found within your pieces.
- Having patterns or marks on a piece that you can recreate and continue past the piece is a great way to add interest and merge pieces even more.
- Spraying, or dripping inks onto your spread creates a unifying layer across the pieces.

STEP 4: As your collage background develops start thinking about where you would like to place your focal point and about how your background and focal image are going to interact. For example, if your image is light perhaps create a darker area within your spread where your figure is going to be placed to create contrast and to help draw your viewer's eye toward your focal point.

STEP 5: Once you are happy with your background you can add your focal point and any final details you would like to form part of your final layer. For this spread, I used a figure cut from one of my monoprints as my focal point and then decided to add some hand-cut stars to the background which felt like a night sky. Stars very often represent hope and wonder within my work.

Make it your own

This layering technique can be used to create so many variations. Your colors, marks, focal points, and final details all add to your collage landscape and the story imagined by your viewers. Have fun and let your imagination run wild.

"More is more
+ less is a bore"
- IRIS APFEL

VANESSA'S TAKE

Still
growing
through
what I go
through

CAYLEE'S TAKE:

yes

YOUR TAKE:

LESSON FIVE:
Peel + Reveal

ALLOW THE UNEXPECTED TO GUIDE YOUR FLOW TO REVEAL
WHAT LIES BENEATH

This method is one where we really let things happen out
of our control. We will be gluing down a set of images
in multiple layers. Then we will peel, pull, rip and rub
some of the papers to reveal what lies underneath. This is
a process that lets you play with your intuition, forces
you to see that there are no mistakes and
takes your interaction with the page to
another level.

ART TEACHER:
VANESSA OLIVER-LLOYD

CORE TECHNIQUE:
Layering papers and then
rubbing / peeling /tearing
them to reveal what is
under the layers

Ingredients

- Your journal
- A selection of papers including vintage text pages, magazine images, book pages, tissue paper, mulberry paper, washi paper.
- Matte medium
- Brush for matte medium
- Water
- Scissors
- Glue stick

Method

STEP 1: Pick a selection of papers to use. Glossy paper works best although I did get some very interesting results with an old book page that wasn't glossy. You need a paper that can withstand some rubbing. Add in a couple of thinner papers for transparency like mulberry paper or tissue paper. Japanese washi paper is also great for this. Pay attention to the colors and style of imagery so that you can match the images with the message you are trying to convey.

STEP 2: Start by laying down your images without gluing. Simply see how you would like to arrange the images. Move things around until you have something you like. There will be images that are going to be covered up by the second layer, so think about what you want to be revealed using the method we will apply.

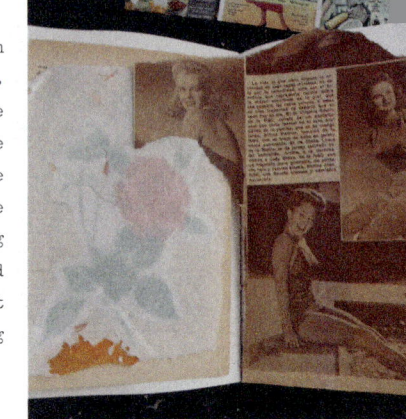

STEP 3: Once you have a good handle on how you will layer the images, start gluing. You will need to use matte medium for this step because it seals in the papers. Use matte medium on both sides of the papers you are putting down. Once the first layer is down, let everything dry for as long as possible; 24 hours is the best. I did 6 hours of drying time.

STEP 4: Now we add the second layer of images using the matte medium. Notice I left some parts of the papers sticking up, not glued down. Those will be fun to peel when we get to the second part of this lesson. Let everything dry 1-2 hours.

STEP 5: Get a small bowl of water. Wet one of the papers that sits on top - for me it is this German text page that I adhered upside down - by dipping your finger in the water and then starting to gently rub the page. Be patient and take your time. Keep rubbing the same spot. Slowly but surely, the fibers of the paper will break down and you will start to reveal the image that is underneath.

STEP 6: In my case, you can see the woman's face with the underside of the typeface on top of her features. Slowly widen the space you are revealing by adding water and rubbing off the paper fibers. Be careful not to rub too hard or go too far because you will rub off the layer that is being revealed.

37

Take a break from rubbing the same area by pulling and peeling off other bits of paper around your spread. Do this as boldly as you can!

STEP 7: Here is where I should have stopped rubbing. I ended up going too far and lost the woman's face. But what appeared was a pair of shoes and that fit in really nicely with what I am trying to say here.

STEP 8: Go around your page and peel off anything that isn't stuck down, starting with the bottom layer. Incorporate these smaller peeled pieces into your collage.

Let the process guide this dialogue with the page: as you peel there are things that you won't like or that don't look how you wanted them to. This allows you to engage fully with your spread and immerse yourself in this method by bringing it back to something you like. You can add as many layers as you want to this.

STEP 9: *Details:* I love how the mulberry paper I used turned into a transparency in some places and covered up the features in others.

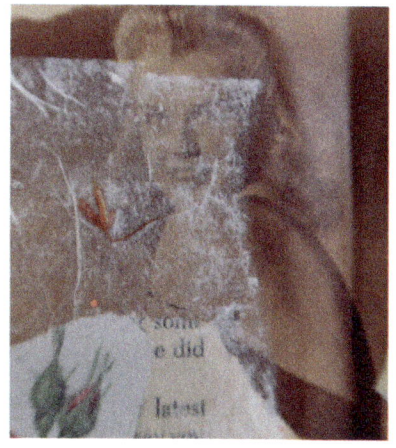

When you are happy with how the spread looks, add some bold words to reveal (if only to yourself) what the message of this spread is.

Make it your own

The easiest way of making this yours is through your choice of images. What are you trying to say? What needs to be revealed under the top layers? What is the deeper message? How can you roll with how the page unfolds - or reveals itself - and still express what you are needing to?

CLAUDETTE'S TAKE:

CAYLEE'S TAKE:

YOUR TAKE:

LESSON SIX:
Layering Transparencies

PLAY WITH PAPERS OF VARYING OPACITIES

Without a doubt, this is my favorite current technique in art journaling. Playing with transparent and semi-transparent elements makes for such a fun spread.

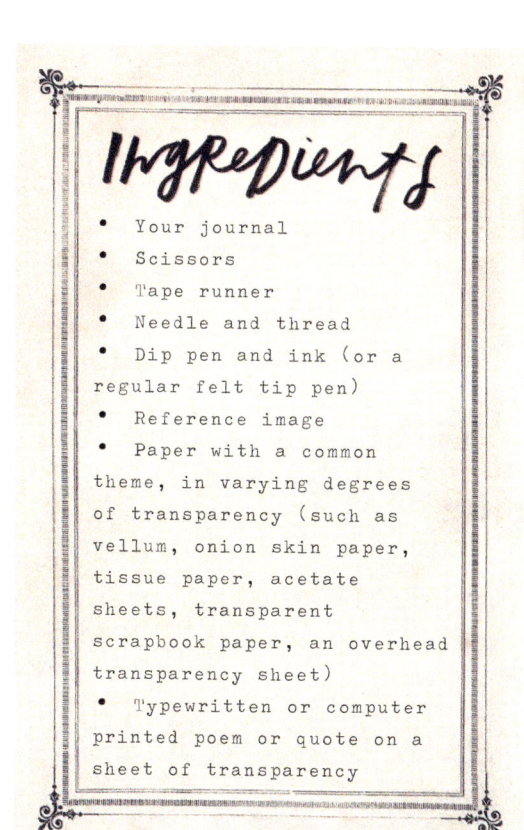

Ingredients

- Your journal
- Scissors
- Tape runner
- Needle and thread
- Dip pen and ink (or a regular felt tip pen)
- Reference image
- Paper with a common theme, in varying degrees of transparency (such as vellum, onion skin paper, tissue paper, acetate sheets, transparent scrapbook paper, an overhead transparency sheet)
- Typewritten or computer printed poem or quote on a sheet of transparency

ART TEACHER:
CAYLEE GREY

CORE TECHNIQUE:
Layering with ephemera with varying opacities

Method

STEP 1: Use a dip pen and ink to draw a motif onto vellum. If you're using the Get Messy Art Journal, you can use one of the sheets with vellum as long as the page behind it is clear. While drawing, put your reference image behind the vellum and loosely trace. To avoid copying the image entirely, keep your drawing loose.

STEP 2: Fussy cut the drawing from the vellum. If the vellum is a page in your journal, keep the side that touches the center intact. Cut about an inch away from the center to create a little flap so that the page stays in the journal. If you're using a sheet of vellum, cut right around it.

STEP 3: Add your most opaque piece of paper, something more on the neutral side to cover the base of your page.

STEP 4: If you're using the Get Messy Art Journal: glue the strip of vellum down and leave your image.

STEP 5: Add more paper as strips.

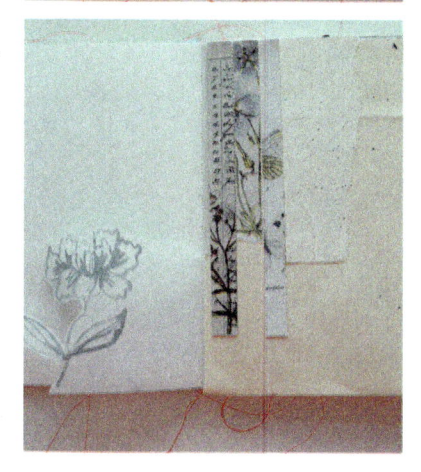

STEP 6: Glue one edge of your poem and use one of the strips to glue down on top of it to hide the visible glue

STEP 7: Using your needle and thread, thread your drawing to your page. I love Xs.

If your vellum is particularly thick, you can pre-punch your holes with a needle or awl to make it easier to sew through.

Make it your own

Use matte medium to glue down your paper (especially with tissue paper - it looks gorgeous). I would never personally do this because matte medium is my sworn enemy - if you're wanting to make it yours too, you can try playing with wet medium

CLAUDETTE'S TAKE:

VANESSA'S TAKE:

YOUR TAKE:

BONUS:

Collage as Expression

Here's some bonus inspiration from
an artist currently rocking COLLAGE in her work.

FEATURED ARTIST:
ALYSSA GRIESE

Collage is a wonderful technique to use in your journal. I rely heavily on the process of collage to convey certain thoughts and feelings that I need to get out of my head and into my journal. It also allows me to create little worlds in which my feelings can reside. For myself, like many others, I don't have a lot of time to devote to just art time and I find that collage has been an effective use of my creative time. Not only is it utterly satisfying to create something from just bits of paper and glue, but it also allows me to create something quickly that would otherwise take me a long time to paint or draw from scratch. I love when pieces of ephemera come together serendipitously to form something meaningful. I love the entire process of puzzling together bits, ripping apart pieces of paper and gluing them all together again to express something that's been happening inside my brain. The possibilities are endless, the materials are resourceful, and my soul is completely satisfied by the end of it.

the edge of the lake dark and forbidding

Slowly, with no doubt or hesitation

through the open window to the fields

under dead leaves

Printed in Great Britain
by Amazon